W9-BCG-935

I SCREAM NAILS

DIY nail Art

I Scream Nails DIY Nail Art
published in 2015 by Chirpy Bird,
an imprint of Hardie Grant Egmont
Ground Floor, Building 1, 658 Church Street,
Richmond, VIC, 3121, Australia
www.hardiegrantegmont.com.au

All rights reserved. No part of this publication may be reproduced, stored
in a retrieval system or transmitted in any form by any means, electronic,
mechanical, photocopying, recording or otherwise, without the prior written
permission of the publishers and copyright holders.

A CiP record for this title is available from the National Library of Australia.

Text and design copyright © 2015 Hardie Grant Egmont
Illustrations, character art and logo copyright © 2015 I Scream Nails

I Scream Nails character art, logo and illustrations
by Benjamin Johnson (also known as what_the_hello)
Book design by Kristy Lund-White
Nail art by Zinya Langsford, Liam Taylor and Zinta Nowland
Photography by Rachel Lewis

I Scream Nails would like to thank the I Scream Nails team for all their
amazing ongoing hard work and creativity. We would also like to thank our
clients and dedicated I Screamers for their support.

Printed in China by 1010 Printing International Limited

10 9 8 7 6 5 4 3 2 1

CONTENTS

SO COOL!

MEET THE CREW

Drum roll, please! Introducing the masterminds behind the GENIUS nail art in this book ... I Scream Nails!

CELIA

THE BOSS!

Nickname: Cels

Fave nail designs: Definitely a neon rainbow set with crystals.

Fave style of music: Top 40, of course! Anything I can sing along to ...

Inspiration: The I Scream Nails team. Everyone is amazing and talented and works hard at being the best they can. Their design ideas and attitude to their work inspires me to keep working at growing I Scream Nails.

Fave catchphrase: SHAMONE!

ZINYA

Nickname: Ninoosh

Fave nail designs: Our 'Patternation' exhibition nails and the nails I did for fashion label Discount Universe.

Inspiration: 80s and 90s fashion, opulence, gold bling and sparkles.

Finish this sentence: *If I didn't paint nails, I would be* ... painting on a larger scale.

Fave saying: "Less is a snore!" as said by Gianni Versace.

Advice to future nail artists: Get the right tools and practise, practise, practise!

LIAM

Nickname: Liam Peter Rabbit

Fave nail designs: Peter Pan and Little Mermaid designs. Also galaxy nails, houndstooth design and anything with an ombrè. Hot.

Inspiration: My friend and fellow artist, Zinya, inspires me to do well at work. My big sister Laura inspires me the most. She is the best person I know.

Finish this sentence: *If I didn't paint nails, I would be* ... a merman.

Fave catchphrase: "Oh well!" and "that's hot!" – I say these about 127 times a day.

ZINTA

Nickname: Zin or Zinna

Fave nail designs: Fades or sweet mermaid scales.

Inspiration: My parents, my sister Astrid and my boyfriend Simon.

Finish this sentence: *If I didn't paint nails, I would be* ... doing something equally as fun and creative – I hope!

Advice to future nail artists: If you have a passion for it, practise as much as you can.

So cool!

7

TOOLS
OF THE TRADE

These are the bits and pieces you need to paint super-awesome nail art. Don't have a striper tool? Try painting lines with a thin paint brush or toothpick! No dotting tool in your neck of the woods? Give a bobby pin a go! Look in your kitchen, bathroom and pencil case for inspiration.

Cotton buds
for cleaning nail polish drips

Bobby pins
for dots

Dotting tools
for spots and dots

Block buffer
for smooth nails (before base coat)

Scissors
for quick trims

Nail polish for painting

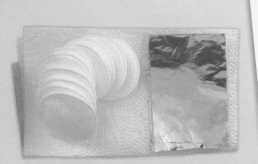

Cotton pads for nail polish removal

Foil for mixing colour. Spread polish here to put on dotting tool.

Build a nail art toolkit over time as your skills grow. With the right tools, your nail art designs will look super-slick and ... wait for it ... POLISHED!

Orange sticks for tidying cuticles and nail drips

Toothpicks for stripes, spots and dots

Striper for straight lines

Skewers for stripes, spots and dots

Nail polish remover for nail polish removal

File for smooth nails

And don't forget ...

Thin paint brush for straight lines and stripes

Kitchen sponges for fades and ombré (gradient) effects

Base coat for prepping nails

Top coat for glossy nails

PREPPING A WORKSPACE

Whether you're painting your own nails or someone else's, you will need your tools in easy reach. Keep your workspace tidy and then you can focus on painting amazing nail art (not searching for a cotton bud)!

The DOs and DON'Ts of Painting Nails

DO

✓ Sit at a table with good light (near a window or lamp).

✓ Keep your workspace clean, organised and comfortable.

✓ Take your time and relax.

DON'T

✗ Paint nails in the dark or on a hammock.

✗ Paint nails over white carpet or while wearing a wedding gown.

✗ Paint nails and eat pizza at the same time.

SO COOL!

FACING OUT

When painting your nail designs, the design will often 'face out'. Look at these examples to see what we mean! This means that the nail artist – that's you! – isn't working upside down like a fruit bat.

PREPARE,
PAINT AND PERFECT

Looking good!

1
PREPARE

- Remove old nail polish with nail polish remover.

- File nails to an even length.

- Gently roughen the nail surface with a buffer.

12

2 PAINT

BASE COAT

- Apply thin layer of clear base coat.
- Use three swift strokes (or lines) to cover the nail. Paint from the base to the tip.
- Allow base coat to dry.

POLISH

- Put a small amount of nail polish on your brush. If the nail polish drips, you have used WAY too much!
- Use three swift strokes (or lines) to cover the nail with colour. Paint from the base to the tip and apply polish evenly.
- Allow nail polish to dry before adding another coat or colour.

3 PERFECT

- ALWAYS seal your nail polish (or nail art) with a top coat.

KNOW YOUR NAIL

Nail tip

Nail base

Nail

Cuticle

LET'S GET
STARTED!

FROGS

It's not easy being green ... unless you're talking about these frogs. This amphibian-themed nail design is crazy cute and not too difficult. HOP TO IT!

Hop! Hop! Hooray!

I SCREAM RATING:

... A BIT TRICKY! ...

LET'S DO IT!

1 Paint two coats of white for the base.

2 Paint a green semicircle at the nail tip.

3 Paint two green dots at the base of the semicircle. Use large dotting tool or bobby pin.

4 Paint two pink dots beneath the two green dots. Use large dotting tool or bobby pin.

5 Paint a black dot inside one of the green dots. Use medium dotting tool or bobby pin.

6 Paint a sideways V inside the other green dot. Use striper, brush or toothpick.

7 Paint a smiley mouth between the pink cheeks. Use striper, brush or toothpick.

TOP COAT!

FLAMINGOS

Use show-stopping shades of candy, magenta and bubblegum to paint this seriously FLA-MAZING flamingo flock.

Flamingo a-go-go!

I SCREAM RATING:

FUN CHALLENGE!

LET'S DO IT!

1 Paint two coats of light blue for the base.

2 Paint a hot pink semicircle at the nail tip.

3 Paint one hot pink dot under the semicircle. Leave a little space.

4 Paint a curved hot pink line to connect the dot and semicircle.

5 Paint a smaller light pink semicircle at the nail tip.

6 Paint a curved black beak. Use striper, brush or toothpick.

7 Paint a white dot on the head. Use medium dotting tool or bobby pin.

8 Paint a black dot inside the white dot. Use small dotting tool or toothpick.

TOP COAT!

CLOUDS

Cumulus? Cirrus? Cumulonimbus?
We're not sure, but these clouds are the
perfect nail design for a rainy day.
The sponged violet-blue base
forms a hazy sky.

Dreamy!

I SCREAM
RATING:

... A BIT TRICKY! ...

LET'S DO IT!

1 Paint two coats of light blue for the base.

2 Paint a violet line and a blue line on a small square of kitchen sponge.

3 Gently dab the sponge over the nail, moving from left to right. The violet and blue should blend horizontally.

4 Clean the outer edges of the nail with a cotton bud lightly dipped in nail polish remover.

5 Overlap white dots to build a cloud shape. Use large dotting tool or bobby pin.

6 Repeat this process to create a fluffy cloud.

7 Fill nail with fluffy clouds.

TOP COAT!

WILD STRAWBERRIES

Wild strawberries! TASTE-TASTIC!
This nail design is 'berry' sweet
and 'berry' delightful – just
like the real thing!

So sweet!

I SCREAM
RATING:

EASY!

LET'S DO IT!

 **1** Paint two coats of red for the base.

 2 Paint green zigzags at the nail tip.

 **3** Fill in the zigzags with green to create a leafy top.

 **4** Paint yellow dots across the nail. Try to make the dots an oval shape. Use small dotting tool or toothpick.

 **5** Add another row of yellow dots. Use small dotting tool or toothpick.

 **TOP COAT!**

OMG!
CHOCOLATE!

TWO HANDS! TEN BLOCKS OF CHOCOLATE! What can we say? This nail design is almost good enough to eat! (Note: Please don't eat your hands.)

nom-nom-nom!

I SCREAM RATING:

••• SUPER CHALLENGE! •••

24

LET'S DO IT!

 **1** Paint two coats of brown for the base.

 **2** Paint three black vertical lines spaced evenly across the nail. It's easier if you start with the middle stripe! Use striper, brush or toothpick.

 **3** Paint four black horizontal lines to form a grid. Use striper, brush or toothpick.

 **4** Paint a light tan L-shape inside each square. Use striper, brush or toothpick.

 **5** Paint a dark brown L-shape inside each square (opposite the light tan L-shape). Use striper, brush or toothpick.

TOP COAT!

CREATIVE SPACE:
ANIMALS

Got a fave animal or a much-loved pet?
Maybe you REALLY like the jungle or
rainforest! Use these pages to design
nail art based on animals and pets.

SO
COOL!

wow!

27

CRAZY!

TOTALLY AWESOME!

31

I SCREAM
NAILS-O-SAURUS

The I Scream Nails-O-Saurus is our very own prehistoric discovery: it's a cross between a stegosaurus and a brachiosaurus. No-one really knows what shade dinosaurs were, so you don't have to stick to green!

GRRRREAT!

I SCREAM RATING:

FUN CHALLENGE!

LET'S DO IT!

1 Paint two coats of purple for the base.

2 Paint a bright green rounded L-shape from the nail tip.

3 Paint a dark green zigzag on the outside of the L-shape. Use striper, brush or toothpick.

4 Fill in the zigzag. Use striper, brush or toothpick.

5 Paint a white dot on the dinosaur's head. This is the dinosaur's eyeball! Use medium dotting tool or bobby pin.

6 Paint a black dot inside the white eyeball. Use small dotting tool or toothpick.

7 Paint a black zigzag for the dinosaur's mouth. Use striper, brush or toothpick.

TOP COAT!

EYE! EYE!

These eyeballs look soooooooo easy, but they need a super-steady hand to get an even shape. With a bit of practice, you'll have perfect peepers! Our eyes are blue, but try brown, green or hazel.

Here's lookin' at ya!

I SCREAM RATING:

... SUPER CHALLENGE! ...

LET'S DO IT!

1 Paint two coats of light pink for the base.

2 Paint a white eye shape in the middle of the nail. Use striper or nail polish brush.

3 Paint a light blue circle in the centre of the eye shape. Use large dotting tool or nail polish brush.

4 Paint a black dot in the centre of the light blue circle. Use medium dotting tool or bobby pin.

5 Paint around the white eye shape to create an outline. Use striper or brush.

6 Paint thin black lines radiating from the eye (these are the eyelashes). Use striper or brush.

7 Paint a white dot on the blue circle to make the eye twinkle. Use small dotting tool or toothpick.

TOP COAT!

I SCREAM
FOR ICE-CREAMS!

I scream, you scream, we all scream for
ICE-CREAMS. We've chosen a pink ice-cream,
but you could go with almost any shade (green
for pistachio? Orange for mango? Brown for
chocolate?) Whatever you choose, add
sprinkles and a cherry on top.

That's cool!

No, it's HOT!

I SCREAM RATING:

··· A BIT TRICKY! ···

LET'S DO IT!

 **1** Paint two coats of tan on the top half of the nail (from the middle to the tip).

 **2** Paint a brown crisscross grid over the tan base. This is the ice-cream cone! Use striper, brush or toothpick.

 **3** Paint pink dots near the top of the cone to create a line. Use medium dotting tool or bobby pin.

 **4** Paint the rest of the nail pink.

 **5** Paint a big red dot near the cuticle. This ice-cream has a cherry on top! Use medium dotting tool or bobby pin.

 **6** Paint small multicoloured dots over the pink. These are candy sprinkles! Use small dotting tool or toothpick.

 TOP COAT!

CUPCAKES

Who doesn't go cray-cray for cupcakes?
With ten cupcakes on your hands, you have
a CUPCAKE PARTY. We have used white
polish for frosting. You could use
different shades and create
a cupcake rainbow!

Let's party!

I SCREAM RATING:

A BIT TRICKY!

LET'S DO IT!

1 Paint two coats of pink on the top half of the nail (from the middle to the tip).

2 Paint dark pink vertical stripes over the light pink base. This is the 'cup' for your 'cupcake'! Use striper, brush or toothpick.

3 Paint white dots near the top of the 'cup' to create a line. Use medium dotting tool or bobby pin.

4 Paint the rest of the nail white.

5 Paint a big red dot near the cuticle. This is a 'cherry'! Use medium dotting tool or bobby pin.

6 Paint small multicoloured dots over the pink. These are candy sprinkles! Use small dotting tool or toothpick.

TOP COAT!

SMILEYS

Yellow smiley faces are a design CLASSIC. We like our faces happy, but you can change your smiley's mood from glad to sad with a stroke of the brush!

I'm happy!

I SCREAM RATING:

SUPER SIMPLE!

LET'S DO IT!

1 Paint two coats of yellow for the base.

2 Paint two black dots for eyes. Use medium dotting tool or bobby pin.

3 Paint a short line under each eye. Use striper, brush or toothpick.

4 Connect the lines with a smiley mouth. Use striper, brush or toothpick.

Experiment to create different expressions.

TOP COAT!

41

CREATIVE SPACE:
FOOD

Do you go cray-cray for pizza? Maybe you are OBSESSED with doughnuts! Use these pages to design nail art based on your fave foods.

SO COOL!

wow!

CRAZY!

45

TOTALLY AWESOME!

47

BUNNIES

One bunny is crazy-cute, but ten bunnies is A CUTENESS INVASION! We've chosen a sugary shade of pink for our bunnies, but any hue would be just as sweet.

Awwwww!

I SCREAM RATING:

FUN CHALLENGE!

LET'S DO IT!

1 Paint two coats of light pink for the base.

2 Paint two ears in neon pink. Use brush or striper. We've made one ear floppy.

3 Paint two black eyes. Use medium dotting tool or bobby pin.

4 Paint a tiny black nose between the eyes. Use small dotting tool or toothpick.

5 Paint a curvy black mouth. Use striper, brush or toothpick.

6 Add eyelashes. Use striper, brush or toothpick.

7 Paint five blue dots in a small circle over the straight ear. Use medium dotting tool or bobby pin.

8 Paint a yellow dot inside the blue circle of dots. Use small dotting tool or bobby pin. Now you have a flower!

9 Paint four white dots to make the eyes twinkle. Use striper, brush or toothpick.

TOP COAT!

KAWAII CLOUD

'Kawaii' is Japanese for 'cute'.
Nothing gets much cuter than this
smiling cloud at the end of a rainbow!

Cute!
Cute!
Cute!

I SCREAM
RATING:

A BIT TRICKY!

LET'S DO IT!

 **1** Paint two coats of light blue for the base.

 **2** Paint a curved red line from the corner of the cuticle to the middle of the nail. Use striper or nail polish brush.

 **3** Repeat step 2 using yellow and then green to create a rainbow.

4 Paint a curved line of white dots. Use large dotting tool or bobby pin.

 **5** Fill in the blue area below the white dots with white polish.

6 Paint two black dots on an angle. These are the cloud's eyes. Use large dotting tool or bobby pin.

 **7** Paint a smiley mouth between the eyes. Use striper, brush or toothpick.

 **8** Paint two white dots in each eye. Use small and medium dotting tools or a toothpick and bobby pin.

TOP COAT!

DOGS

Who let the dogs out? Does anybody know the answer to THAT question? What we do know is you'll have nice paws with these ten doggies.

BOW-WOW!

I SCREAM RATING:

FUN CHALLENGE!

LET'S DO IT!

1 Paint two coats of tan for the base.

2 Paint a white semicircle at the nail tip.

 **3** Paint two dark brown curved stripes either side of the tan base. These are the dog's ears.

 **4** Paint black eyes on the 'border' between the white and tan. Use medium dotting tool or bobby pin. Add a black dot for the nose.

 **5** Paint a black curvy mouth. Add a tongue outline. Use striper or brush.

 **6** Paint a little pink tongue. Use small dotting tool or bobby pin.

 **7** Paint four white dots to make the dog's eyes twinkle.

TOP COAT!

BACK TO THE 90s!

Party time! Excellent! Made up of squiggles, lines, V-shapes and dots, this 90s pattern is, like, totally rad. PEACE OUT!

Whoah! Radical!

I SCREAM RATING:

EASY!

LET'S DO IT!

1  Paint two coats of light pink for the base.

2 Paint a bright pink line and a light pink line on a small square of kitchen sponge.

3  Gently dab the sponge over the nail, moving from left to right. The bright pink and light pink should blend.

4 Clean the outer edges of the nail with a cotton bud lightly dipped in nail polish remover.

5  Paint blue squiggles. Use striper, brush or toothpick.

6 Paint yellow V-shapes. Use striper, brush or toothpick.

7  Paint black parallel lines. Use striper, brush or toothpick.

8 Paint white dots. Use small dotting tool or toothpick.

  TOP COAT!

HERE, KITTY KITTY!

Our kitties are orange like marmalade, but any shade would be PURRRRR-FECT. If you want to show some serious CATTITUDE, paint a rainbow of feline friends!

Totally claw-some!

I SCREAM RATING:

... FUN CHALLENGE! ...

LET'S DO IT!

1 Paint two coats of white for the base.

2 Paint an orange semicircle at the nail tip.

3 Paint two orange triangles at the semicircle base. Use striper or nail polish brush.

4 Paint a white semicircle at the nail tip.

5 Paint a pink triangle inside each orange triangle. Use striper or brush.

6 Paint black eyes on the 'border' between the white and orange semicircles. Use medium dotting tool or bobby pin. Add a small black triangle for the nose with striper or toothpick.

7 Paint a black curvy mouth. Add a tongue outline and whiskers. Use striper, brush or toothpick.

8 Paint a little pink tongue. Use small dotting tool or bobby pin.

9 Paint four white dots to make the kitty's eyes twinkle.

TOP COAT!

CREATIVE SPACE: PATTERNS

Do you have a fave pattern or two? How about dots, spots, checks, stripes, squiggles and swirls? Use these pages to design nail art based on the patterns you love!

SO COOL!

wow!

CRAZY!

61

TOTALLY AWESOME!

63

GET INSPIRED!

Now that you have the skills, try out some of these fresh designs or get inspired to paint more designs of your own. Remember: if you can think it, you can paint it!